Schulz und Schulz
Erlebnismuseum Perlmutter
Adorf/Vogtland

Die Beteiligten an dem Projekt: Ansgar Schulz, Benedikt Schulz, Bürgermeister Rico Schmidt, Museumsleiter Steffen Dietz, wissenschaftliche Museumsmitarbeiterin Sarah Kaiser und Stadtbaumeister Mario Beine (von links nach rechts) auf der Dachrinne des Neubaus. (Photo: Antje Goßler.)

Those involved in the project: Ansgar Schulz, Benedikt Schulz, mayer Rico Schmidt, museum director Steffen Dietz, museum research assistant Sarah Kaiser and city architect Mario Beine (from left to right) on the gutter of the new building. (Photo: Antje Goßler.)

Schulz und Schulz
Erlebnismuseum Perlmutter
Adorf/Vogtland

Im Gespräch/In conversation
Rico Schmidt, Mario Beine, Steffen Dietz,
Sarah Kaiser, Ansgar Schulz, Benedikt Schulz

Baubeschreibung/Building description
Ansgar Schulz, Benedikt Schulz

Photographien/Photographs
Gustav Willeit

Edition Axel Menges

ISBN 978-3-86905-050-8

Druck und Bindearbeiten/Printing and binding: Graspo CZ, a. s., Zlın, Tschechische Republik/ Czech Republic

Lektorat/Editorial work: Dorothea Duwe
Gestaltung/Design: Axel Menges

Edition Axel Menges GmbH
Esslinger Straße 24
DE-70736 Fellbach
www.AxelMenges.de
AxelMenges@aol.com

6 Bürgermeister Rico Schmidt, Stadtbaumeister Mario Beine, Museumsleiter Steffen Dietz und die wissenschaftliche Museumsmitarbeiterin Sarah Kaiser im Gespräch mit Ansgar Schulz und Benedikt Schulz
10 Ansgar und Benedikt Schulz: Das Erlebnismuseum Perlmutter in Adorf / Vogtland

12 Ortungsplan der Stadt Adorf
12 Lageplan des Museums
14 Grundrisse
15 Schnitte und Aufriß der Nordseite
16 Gesamtansicht von Nordwesten
18 Detailansichten von Nordwesten
20 Detailansichten des neuen Baukörpers
22 Detailansicht von Osten
23 Detailansicht von Westen
24 Der Zugang zum Museum
26 Das Foyer
28 Der Museumsshop
30 Der Patio
32 Die Garderobe
33 Die Treppe in die Obergeschosse
34 Ausstellungen im Altbau

40 Datenblatt

7 Mayor Rico Schmidt, city architect Mario Beine, museum director Steffen Dietz and the museum research assistant Sarah Kaiser in conversation with Ansgar Schulz and Benedikt Schulz
11 Ansgar and Benedikt Schulz: The Mother-of-Pearl Experience Museum in Adorf / Vogtland

12 Location map of the town of Adorf
12 Site plan of the museum
14 Floor plans
15 Sections and elevation of the north side
16 General view from the north-west
18 Detailed views from the north-west
20 Detailed views of the body of the new building
22 Detailed view from the east
23 Detailed view from the west
24 The access to the museum
26 The foyer
28 The museum shop
30 The patio
32 The cloakroom
33 The stairs leading to the upper floors
34 Exhibitions in the old building

40 Fact sheet

Bürgermeister Rico Schmidt (RS), Stadtbaumeister Mario Beine (MB), Museumsleiter Steffen Dietz (SD) und die wissenschaftliche Museumsmitarbeiterin Sarah Kaiser (SK) im Gespräch mit Ansgar Schulz (AS) und Benedikt Schulz (BS)

AS In Adorfs Geschichte gab es eine Blütezeit. Wie würden Sie diese beschreiben?
SD Adorf ist die älteste Stadt des Oberen Vogtlands, eine Ackerbürgerstadt, die sich im 19. Jahrhundert zum Industrieort entwickelt hat, mit zwei Schwerpunkten: die Textilindustrie als großer Arbeitgeber, aber auch die Perlmutterwarenherstellung.
AS Welche Produkte hat die Perlmutterindustrie aus dem Material hergestellt?
SD Körperschmuck, in erster Linie für Frauen, zum Beispiel Ketten, Broschen, Anhänger, dazu Raum- und Tafelschmuck, Gegenstände, die zur Verzierung des Raumes dienen, sowie Schmuckschatullen und Schachbretter. Oder Schiffsmodelle, die als Souvenirartikel für die Bäder an Nord- und Ostsee gedacht waren. Eine sehr, sehr breite Produktpalette und mit weltweitem Export bis nach Amerika.
BS Wie viele Einwohner hat Adorf, und wie ist die demographische Situation?
RS Etwa 4.600, Tendenz weiter fallend, da wir einen hohen Altersdurchschnitt haben und eine zu geringe Geburtenrate. Uns fehlt eine komplette Generation mitsamt deren Kindern, die nach der Wende weggegangen ist.
BS Leidet die Gemeinde unter der Abwanderung der jüngeren Bevölkerung?
MB Ja wir leiden schon noch, weil wir nach wie vor Einwohner verlieren. Das ist aber nicht nur in Adorf so, sondern im gesamten Vogtland. Positiv steht dem gegenüber, daß es auch Rückkehrer gibt, die jetzt ins Rentenalter kommen.
AS Das hört man öfter. Viele Menschen verlassen die teuren Ballungszentren, wenn sie in die Rente kommen.
RS Es kehren aber auch Jüngere zurück, weil hier die Eltern und Großeltern wohnen. Sie haben Kinder bekommen und finden bei uns eine gute Kinderversorgung vor. Wir haben Kindergärten und Schulen, und dann natürlich das, was im Vogtland getan wird, um die Region für alle Generationen attraktiv zu machen.
BS Welche Projekte verfolgte und verfolgt Adorf, um dem demographischen Wandel entgegenzuwirken?
MB Die Infrastruktur muß passen. Wir müssen unser Straßennetz in Ordnung halten, aber viel wichtiger ist die Bildungsinfrastruktur. Und da ist in den letzten Jahren in Adorf viel getan worden. Wir haben zwei Kinderkrippen, eine Tagesmutter, zwei Kindergärten, eine Grundschule, eine Oberschule und auch eine eigene Musikschule. Im Umkreis gibt es mehrere Oberschulen und Gymnasien.
RS Es ist auch in die Stadtentwicklung investiert worden. Wir führen viele Projekte durch, um auf Adorf aufmerksam zu machen, mit Festen, Veranstaltungen, Musikabenden, so daß aus der Region und überregional viele Leute hierherkommen. Wir nehmen an Wettbewerben teil, haben auch schon einige Preise gewonnen. Mit dem Erlebnismuseum Perlmutter setzen wir jetzt einen Leuchtturm, der auf den Tourismus abzielt. Bisher fahren die Menschen durch Adorf hindurch, um zum Beispiel nach Bad Elster oder Markneukirchen zu gelangen. Das soll sich ändern.
SD Es geht uns auch um einen Imagewandel für Adorf. Bad Elster steht für die Bäderkultur, Markneukirchen für das feine Handwerk, und Adorf war die Arbeiterstadt mit den großen Arbeitgebern Reichsbahn, Halbmond-Teppichwerke und Vowetex, den Vogtländischen Webereitextilien. Doch seit 1990 ist das im Wandel. Adorf kann und muß einen anderen Ruf bekommen.
BS Was hält die Bevölkerung in Vogtland/Adorf zusammen? Wie würden Sie die Identität der Adorfer beschreiben?

1. Adorf von Nordwesten. (Photo:Albrecht Voß.)

1. Adorf from the north-west. (Photo:Albrecht Voß.)

Mayor Rico Schmidt (RS), city architect Mario Beine (MB), museum director Steffen Dietz (SD) and the museum research assistant Sarah Kaiser (SK) in conversation with Ansgar Schulz (AS) and Benedikt Schulz (BS)

AS There was a golden age in Adorf's history. How would you describe it?
SD Adorf is the oldest town in the Upper Vogtland region, a farming town that developed into an industrial town with two main points in the 19th century, the textile industry as the major employer, but also the mother-of-pearl manufacturing.
AS What products did the mother-of-pearl industry make from the material?
SD Body jewellery, primarily for women, such as necklaces, brooches and pendants, in addition room and table decorations, items used to decorate rooms, as well as jewellery boxes and chessboards. Or model ships, which were intended as souvenirs for the seaside resorts on the North Sea and Baltic Sea. A very, very wide range of products, exported worldwide as far as America.
BS How many inhabitants does Adorf have, and what is the demographic situation?
RS About 4,600, and the trend is continuing to fall, as we have a high average age and a low birth rate. We are missing an entire generation including their children that left after reunification.
BS Is the community suffering from the exodus of the younger population?
MB Yes, we are still suffering because we are continuing to lose residents. However, this is not only the case in Adorf, but throughout the Vogtland region. On the positive side, there are also returnees who are now reaching retirement age.
AS Yes, you hear that a lot. Many people leave the expensive urban centers when they retire.
RS Younger people are also returning because their parents and grandparents live here. They have had children and find good childcare facilities here. We have nurseries and schools, and then, of course, there is what is being done in the Vogtland region to make it attractive for all generations.
BS What projects has Adorf pursued and is pursuing to counteract demographic change?
MB The infrastructure has to be right. We have to keep our road network in good condition, but much more important is the educational infrastructure. And a lot has been done in Adorf in recent years. We have two crèches, a childminder, two nurseries, a primary school, a secondary school and our own music school. There are several secondary schools and grammar schools in the surrounding area.
RS Investments have also been made in urban development. We organise many projects to draw attention to Adorf, with festivals, events and music evenings, so that many people from the region and beyond come here. We take part in competitions and have already won several prizes. With the Mother-of-Pearl Experience Museum, we are now setting a beacon that targets tourism. Until now, people have driven through Adorf to get to Bad Elster or Markneukirchen, for example. That is set to change.
SD We are also interested in changing Adorf's image. Bad Elster stands for spa culture, Markneukirchen for fine craftsmanship, and Adorf was the working-class town with major employers such as Reichsbahn, Halbmond-Teppichwerke and Vowetex, the Vogtland weaving textiles company. But since 1990, this has been changing. Adorf can and must gain a different reputation.
BS What keeps the population in Vogtland/Adorf together? How would you describe the identity of the people of Adorf?

SD Das Kleine, Gemütliche. Jeder kennt jeden. Dieser Zusammenhalt wird auch deutlich in der Vereinsarbeit, die schon immer besonders intensiv war und die nach außen dringt durch die vielen Veranstaltungen, die von den Vereinen organisiert werden.

RS Es ist ein Miteinander zwischen Verwaltung, Bürgerschaft, Vereinen und allen Akteuren im Gewerbe. Dieses Miteinander wollen wir versuchen noch zu stärken.

AS Wie ist es aus dieser Atmosphäre heraus zur Idee des Erlebnismuseums Perlmutter gekommen?

SD Das Museum besteht seit 1955 als kleines Heimatmuseum. Zur Wende war mir bewußt, daß das Heimatmuseum dem Wandel der Gesellschaftsordnung zum Opfer fallen könnte. Deswegen wollte ich einen Schwerpunkt setzen. Schwerpunkte in der Stadtgeschichte waren Textil oder Perlmutter. Eine Textilgeschichte hatte auch der Nachbarort Oelsnitz, also entschied ich mich, zum Thema Perlmutter zu forschen und eine Sammlung aufzubauen. Gemeinsam mit dem heutigen Bürgermeister und den Stadträten reifte schließlich der Gedanke des Erlebnismuseums.

AS Was erhofft sich Adorf von dem neuen Museum?

SD Zum einen die Weiterentwicklung des Museums, bessere Arbeitsbedingungen und vor allem eine viel bessere Ausstellung mit viel mehr Inhalt für die Besucher. Das zweite ist die Stadtentwicklung, über die wir schon gesprochen haben.

AS Gibt es woanders bereits ein solches Perlmutter-Museum?

SD In Deutschland definitiv nicht. Es gibt ein Muscheln-Schnecken-Museum oder Museen, die einfach die Vielfalt der Mollusken darstellen. Aber diese Kombination zwischen Flußperlmuschel, Perlenfischerei und Verarbeitung, die Kombination zwischen Naturschutz und Kunsthandwerk ist einmalig.

AS Es gibt Projekte zur Wiederansiedlung der Muscheln, doch darüber wird nicht viel berichtet. Niemand weiß, wo das ist, oder?

SK Berechtigterweise. Die Perle, die ab und zu in einer Muschel steckt, weckt gewisse Begehrlichkeiten. Um die Muschelbestände zu schützen, hält man die Sache eher bedeckt. Seit 2003 wird das Schutzprojekt samt Renaturierung der Fließgewässer im Vogtland betrieben und versucht, die Muschel vor dem Aussterben zu retten. Im Vogtland war die Art zum Glück noch nicht ausgestorben, weil sie im siedlungsarmen innerdeutschen Grenzgebiet akzeptable Bedingungen vorfand. Die Nachzucht der Flußperlmuschel ist aufwendig und langwierig, aber es gibt erste Erfolge, und tausende Muscheln wurden bereits nachgezüchtet.

BS Interessant, die Muschel verdankt ihr Überleben der deutschen Teilung. Wer finanziert die Wiederansiedlung?

SD Früher der Freistaat Sachsen. Seit 2015 ist es in einem Bundesprogramm, manchmal unter Einbeziehung temporärer Förderungen. Wir liefern als Museum auch Zuarbeiten zu Anträgen. Vor allem aber sehen wir uns als Vermittler. Wir versuchen, die Bevölkerung für das Thema zu sensibilisieren. In Gebieten, deren Bedingungen günstig für das Einsetzen der Muscheln sind, wird der Bevölkerung Rücksicht abverlangt, sowohl was die Landwirtschaft als auch was den privaten Bereich betrifft.

BS Das Museum hat also auch einen Aufklärungsauftrag für die Zukunft der Muschel?

SK Ja, und unser Anliegen können wir mit dem neuen Museum viel besser verwirklichen. Wir konnten eine immersive Ausstellung aufbauen, in welche die Besuchenden eintauchen und sich bestenfalls selbst wie eine kleine Muschel fühlen. Zudem können wir das Schutzprojekt der Öffentlichkeit vorstellen und im Bereich der Umweltbildung tätig werden.

2, 3. Ausstellungsexponate.(Photos: Albrecht Voß.)

2, 3. Exhibition objects. (Photo: Albrecht Voß.)

SD The small, cosy community. Everyone knows everyone. This cohesion is also evident in the work of the clubs, which has always been very intensive and is reflected in the many events organised by the clubs.
RS It is a cooperation between municipal administration, citizens, associations and all actors in the trade. We want to try to strengthen this collaboration even further.
AS How did the idea for the Mother-of-Pearl Experience Museum come about in this atmosphere?
SD The museum has existed since 1955 as a small local-history museum. At the time of reunification, I was aware that the local-history museum could fall victim to the changing social order. That's why I wanted to set a focus. The main focuses in the town's history were textiles and mother-of-pearl. The neighbouring town of Oelsnitz also had a history of textiles, so I decided to research the topic of mother-of-pearl and build up a collection. Together with the current mayor and the town councillors, the idea of an interactive museum finally took shape.
AS What does Adorf hope to gain from the new museum?
SD On the one hand, the further development of the museum, better working conditions and, above all, a much better exhibition with much more content for visitors. The second is urban development, which we have already talked about.
AS Is there already a mother-of-pearl museum like this somewhere else?
SD Definitely not in Germany. There is a shell and snail museum, or museums that simply showcase the diversity of molluscs. But this combination of river pearl mussels, pearl fishing and processing, the combination of nature conservation and arts and crafts, is unique.
AS There are projects to reintroduce the mussels, but not much is reported about them. Nobody knows where that is, right?
SK And rightly so. The pearl that occasionally lies hidden in a mussel arouses certain desires. In order to protect mussel stocks, the matter is kept rather under wraps. Since 2003, a conservation project involving the renaturation of watercourses in the Vogtland region has been underway, attempting to save the mussel from extinction. Fortunately, the species had not yet died out in the Vogtland region because it found acceptable conditions in the sparsely populated inner-German border area. Breeding river pearl mussels is a complex and lengthy process, but initial successes have been achieved and thousands of mussels have already been bred.
BS Interesting, the mussel owes its survival to the division of Germany. Who is financing the reintroduction?
SD Formerly the Free State of Saxony. Since 2015 it has been part of a federal programme, sometimes with the help of temporary subsidies. As a museum, we also provide support with applications. Above all, however, we see ourselves as mediators. We try to raise awareness of the issue among the population. In areas where conditions are favourable for the mussels to settle, the population is asked to be considerate, both in agriculture and in their private lives.
BS So the museum also has an educational mission for the future of the mussel?
SK Yes, and we can achieve our goal much better with the new museum. We have been able to create an immersive exhibition in which visitors can immerse themselves and, at best, feel like a little mussel themselves. In addition, we can present the conservation project to the public and become active in the field of environmental education.

Ansgar und Benedikt Schulz

Das Erlebnismuseum Perlmutter in Adorf/Vogtland

Die Stadt Adorf kämpft mit den typischen Problemen ländlicher Regionen: Überalterung und Rückgang der Bevölkerung, Attraktivitätsverlust als Wohn- und Arbeitsort und eine daraus resultierende schwierige wirtschaftliche Lage. Die Stadt stemmt sich diesem Wandel mit Verbesserungen von Infrastruktur und Bildungsangeboten entgegen. Das neue Erlebnismuseum Perlmutter stellt ein Leuchtturmprojekt für Ort und Region dar, das Identifikationsobjekt und Motor einer positiven Entwicklung sein soll. An keinem anderen Ort in Deutschland existiert ein derartiges Museum zu Flußperlmuscheln, Perlenfischerei und Perlmutterwarenherstellung, was Adorf als attraktives Alleinstellungsmerkmal für die aktive Gestaltung des Strukturwandels nutzen möchte.

Das Grundstück des Neubaus war eine Brache ohne Qualität im Erscheinungsbild. Die in das Projekt einbezogenen Altbauten, die rund vier Fünftel der Gesamtfläche ausmachen, waren teilweise ungenutzt und drohten zu verfallen. Durch deren Erhalt und Weiternutzung wurde die örtliche Situation stabilisiert und gestärkt. Mit der Intervention entstand ein lebendiger Ort, der sowohl die unmittelbare Umgebung als auch durch die Nähe zu Marktplatz und Rathaus die gesamte Innenstadt aufwertet. Die Integration der historischen Stadtmauer in den Patio des Museums macht die Geschichte der Stadt erlebbar.

Das Erscheinungsbild des Neubaus ist aus dem Aufbau der Muschel abgeleitet: Die rauhe Schale und das kostbare Innere stehen im Kontrast zueinander und bilden dennoch eine Einheit. Die windschief verformte Gebäudehülle ist eine bildliche Transformation der Muschelschale und sendet ein Signal in den öffentlichen Raum. Über die Betonschale fließt kontinuierlich Wasser in einen Brunnen und verweist so auf fließendes Wasser als Lebensgrundlage der Muschel.

Die gekrümmte Fassade des Neubaus besteht aus einer materialminimierten Hyparschale aus Beton. Die Tragkonstruktion der Altbauten wurde mit Vollholz aus heimischen Wäldern verstärkt; auch wurden für Fenster und Möbel heimische Hölzer verwendet. Auf dem Boden des Neubaus liegt Naturstein aus einem nahe gelegenen Steinbruch.

Der Neubau ist sehr kompakt mit geringem umbauten Raum, weil die Geschoßhöhen der Altbauten übernommen wurden. Der hohe Wärmedämmstandard des Neubaus und die innenseitig gedämmte Hülle der Altbauten sowie die wenigen Öffnungen in den Fassaden sorgen für geringe Wärmeverluste, optimierte Sonneneinstrahlung und ein für die Ausstellungsstücke wichtiges konstantes Klima im Inneren. Die unverkleidete Massivkonstruktion des Neubaus sowie die eingesetzten Lehmziegel und Lehmputzflächen im Bestand wirken als thermische Masse und regulieren die Behaglichkeit und Luftfeuchte im Inneren. Die ständige Bewässerung der Fassade verbessert im Sommer das Mikroklima des Ortes durch das Prinzip der Verdunstungskälte.

Die Räume der Gebäudetechnik befinden sich in einem der angrenzenden Altbauten. Heizung und Kühlung erfolgen mittels einer Sole-Wasser-Wärmepumpe, die mit Solarstrom betrieben wird. Die zentrale Lüftung arbeitet mit Wärmerückgewinnung.

Ansgar and Benedikt Schulz

The Mother-of-Pearl Experience Museum in Adorf / Vogtland

The town of Adorf is struggling with the typical problems of rural regions: an ageing and declining population, a loss of attractiveness as a place to live and work, and the resulting difficult economic situation. The town is countering this change with improvements to infrastructure and educational opportunities. The new Mother-of-Pearl Experience Museum is a flagship project for the town and region, intended to be a symbol of identity and a driver of positive development. Nowhere else in Germany is there a museum dedicated to river pearl mussels, pearl fishing and mother-of-pearl production, which Adorf hopes to use as an attractive unique selling point for actively shaping structural change.

The site of the new building was a wasteland with no appeal in terms of appearance. The old buildings included in the project, which make up around four-fifths of the total area, were partly unused and threatened with decay. Their preservation and continued use stabilised and strengthened the local situation. The intervention created a lively place that enhances both the immediate surroundings and, thanks to its proximity to the market square and town hall, the entire city centre. The integration of the historic city wall into the museum's patio brings the city's history to life.

The appearance of the new building is derived from the structure of the shell: the rough shell and precious interior contrast with each other and yet form a unity. The warped building envelope is a pictorial transformation of the shell and sends a signal into the public space. Water flows continuously over the concrete shell into a fountain, referring to flowing water as the basis of life for the shell.

The curved façade of the new building consists of a material-minimised hypar shell made of concrete. The supporting structure of the old buildings was reinforced with solid wood from local forests; local woods were also used for windows and furniture. The floor of the new building is made of natural stone from a nearby quarry.

The new building is very compact with a small enclosed space because the floor heights of the old buildings were retained. The high thermal insulation standard of the new building and the internally insulated envelope of the old buildings, as well as the few openings in the façades, ensure low heat loss, optimised solar gain and a constant indoor climate, which is important for the exhibits. The unclad solid construction of the new building and the clay bricks and clay plaster surfaces used in the existing buildings act as thermal mass and regulate the comfort and humidity inside. The continuous irrigation of the façade improves the microclimate of the site in summer through the principle of evaporative cooling.

The building services rooms are located in one of the adjacent old buildings. Heating and cooling are provided by a brine-water heat pump powered by solar electricity. The central ventilation system operates with heat recovery.

Hamburg
Berlin
DEUTSCHLAND
Leipzig
Dresden
SACHSEN
Adorf
Frankfurt
Prag
TSCHECHIEN
BAYERN
München

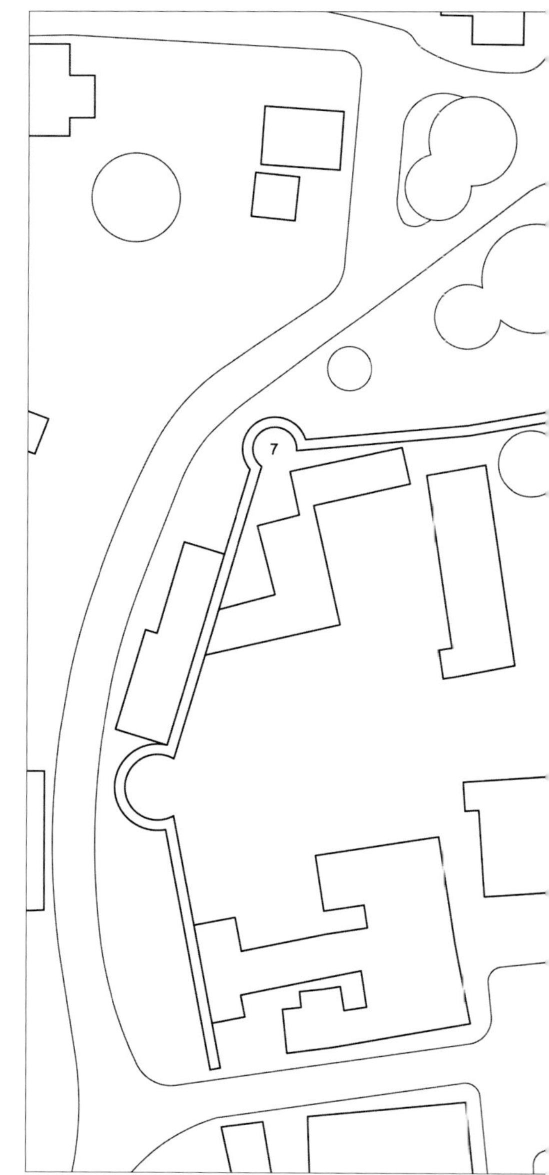
7

1. Ortungsplan der Stadt Adorf.
2. Lageplan des Museums. 1 Sonderausstellung und Museumspädagogik (Neubau), 2 Dauerausstellung (Bestand), 3 Remise (Bestand), 4 Archiv (Bestand), 5 Heimatmuseum und Verwaltung (Bestand Freiberger Tor), 6 St. Johanniskirche, 7 historische Stadtmauer, 8 Marktplatz, 9 Rathaus.

1. Location map of the town of Adorf.
2. Site plan of the museum. 1 temporary exhibition and museum pedagogics (new structure), 2 permanent exhibition (existing structure), 3 carriage shed (existing structure), 4 archive (existing structure), 5 Museum of Local History and administration (existing structure Freiberger Tor), 6 St John's Church, 7 historical town wall, 8 market place, 9 town hall.

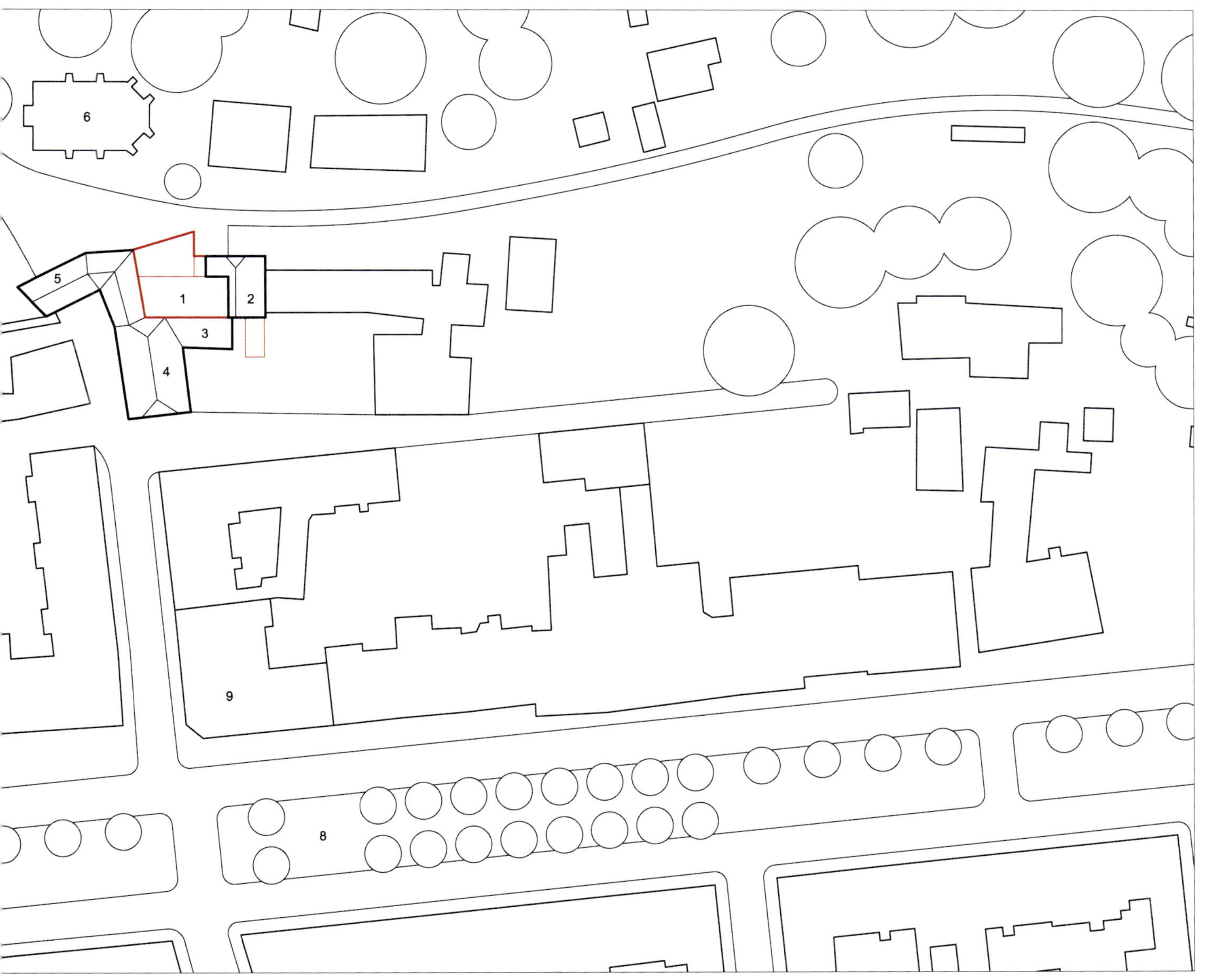

3. Zweites Obergeschoß. 1 Museumspädagogik, 2 Luftraum Patio, 3 Dauerausstellung, 4 Lüftungszentrale, 5 Archiv, 6 Heimatmuseum.

4. Erstes Obergeschoß. 1 Sonderausstellung, 2 Luftraum Patio, 3 Stadtmauer, 4 Dauerausstellung, 5 Technik, 6 Archiv, 7 Besprechung.

5. Erdgeschoß. 1 Wasserbecken, 2 Foyer, 3 Infopoint, 4 Kassenbereich, 5 Museumsshop, 6 Patio, 7 Stadtmauer, 8 Technik, 9 Garderobe, 10 Freiberger Tor (Zugang Verwaltung), 11 Stadttor.

6. Querschnitt. 1 Wasserbecken, 2 Foyer, 3 Patio, 4 Sonderausstellung, 5 Museumspädagogik, 6 Stadtmauer, 7 Technik, 8 Lüftungszentrale, 9 Photovoltaik.

7. Längsschnitt. 1 Kassenbereich und Museumsshop, 2 Foyer, 3 Dauerausstellung, 4 Sonderausstellung, 5 Museumspädagogik, 6 Heimatmuseum, 7 Zugang Verwaltung, 8 Besprechnung, 9 Stadttor.

8. Aufriß von Norden.

3. Second floor. 1 museum pedagogics, 2 airspace of patio, 3 permanent exhibition, 4 ventilation control centre, 5 archive, 6 Museum of Local History.

4. First floor. 1 temporary exhibition, 2 airspace of patio, 3 city wall, 4 permanent exhibition, 5 technical area, 6 archive, 7 meeting.

5. Ground floor. 1 water basin, 2 foyer, 3 info point, 4 ticket office, 5 museum shop, 6 patio, 7 city wall, 8 technical area, 9 cloakroom, 10 Freiberger Tor (access to administration), 11 city gate.

6. Cross section. 1 water basin, 2 foyer, 3 patio, 4 temporary exhibition, 5 museum pedagogics, 6 city wall, 7 technical area, 8 ventilation control centre, 9 photovoltaics.

7. Longitudinal section. 1 ticket office and museum shop, 2 foyer, 3 permanent exhibition, 4 temporary exhibition, 5 museum pedagogics, 6 Museum of Local History, 7 access to administration, 8 meeting, 9 city gate.

8. Elevation from the north.

9
5
8
4
6
7
2
3
1
3
5
6
3
8
4
3
9
7
1
2

S. 16/17
1. Gesamtansicht von Nordwesten mit der St. Johanniskirche im Vordergrund.

2. Ansicht von Nordwesten. Rechts das Heimatmuseum mit dem Freiberger Tor.
3. Der Neubau, eingebettet zwischen den beiden Altbauten. Die Fassade ist eine bildliche Transformation der Muschelschale.

pp. 16/17
1. Overall view from the northwest with St John's Church in the foreground.

2. View from the northwest. On the right is the Museum of Local History with the Freiberger Tor.
3. The new building, embedded between the two old buildings. The façade is a pictorial transformation of a mussel.

4. Detailansicht des Baukörpers des Neubaus mit der schmalen Fensteröffnung im zweiten Obergeschoß.
5. Die Fuge zwischen Alt- und Neubau.

S. 22, 23
6. Detailansicht des Neubaus von Osten. Im Vordergrund der Brunnen.
7. Wasser benetzt permanent die Schale des Neubaus und fließt in einem geregelten Kreislauf in den Brunnen ab.

4. Detailed view of the structure of the new building with the narrow window opening on the second floor.
5. The joint between the old and new buildings.

pp. 22, 23
6. Detailed view of the new building from the east. The fountain in the foreground.
7. Water constantly wets the shell of the new building and flows into the fountain in a regulated cycle.

8, 9. Der Zugang zum Museum liegt unter der auskragenden Fassade des Neubaus.

8, 9. The entrance to the museum is located under the cantilevered façade of the new building.

10. Das Foyer mit Infopoint und Kassenbereich sowie dem Museumsshop dahinter.
11. Das Foyer mit dem Infopoint. Im Hintergrund ein Stück der alten Stadtmauer.

S. 28/29
12. Der Museumsshop.

10. The foyer with information point and ticket office, with the museum shop behind it.
11. The patio with the information point. In the background, a section of the old city wall.

pp. 28/29
12. The museum shop.

500
Teile Puzzle
Freiberger Tor
Freiberger Tor
500

3.6
2.7

S. 30, 31
13. Der Patio mit Blick zurück zum Eingang im Foyer.
14. Der Patio mit der alten Stadtmauer. Er erstreckt sich über alle Geschosse.

15. Die Garderobe mit den Schließfächern.
16. Die Treppe zu den oberen Geschossen mit den Ausstellungen.

pp. 30, 31
13. The patio with a view back to the entrance in the foyer.
14. The patio with the old city wall. It extends over all floors.

15. The cloakroom with the lockers.
16. The staircase to the upper floors with the exhibitions.

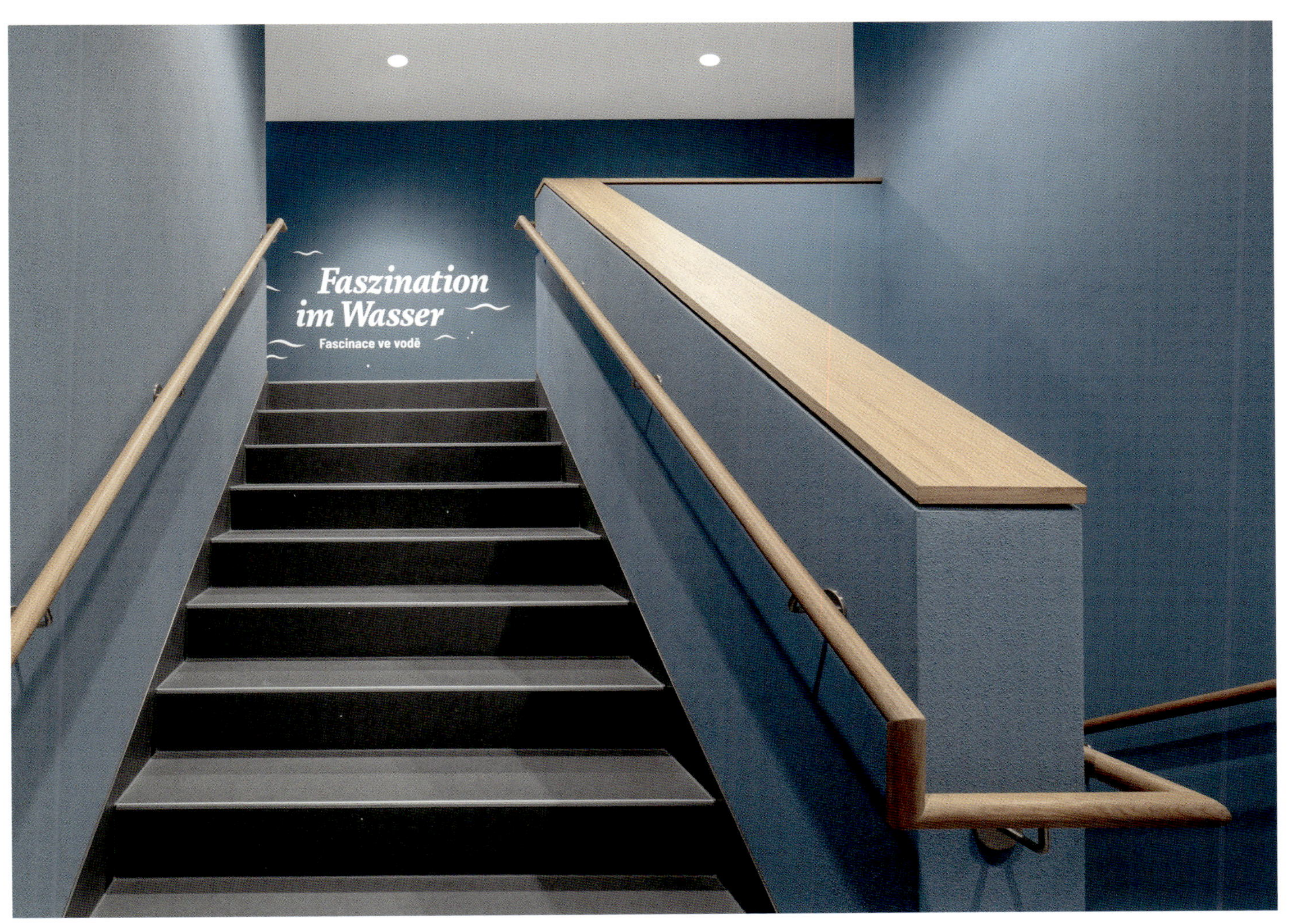

aus
rlmutter
Poklad
z perleti
Der magische Spiegel
Magické zrcadlo

S. 34, 35
17. Der Schatz aus Perlmutter im »Blauen Wunder«.

18. Ausstellung zur Perlenfischerei.
19. Ausstellung zur Perlmutterwarenherstellung.

S. 38/39
20. Adorfer Perlmutter-Glasbilder.

pp. 34, 35
17. The mother-of-pearl treasure in the »Blue Wonder«.

18. Exhibition on pearl fishing.
19. Exhibition on mother-of-pearl production.

pp. 38/39
20. Adorf mother-of-pearl glass pictures.

30
Adorfer Glasbilder
Adorfské skleněné obrázky

Erlebnismuseum Perlmutter
Graben 2
D-08626 Adorf/Vogtland
Tel. +49-37423-2247
museum@adorf-vogtland.de
www.perlmuttermuseum.de

Architekten/Architects

Schulz und Schulz Architekten GmbH
Schwägrichenstraße 13
D-04107 Leipzig
Tel. +49-341-487133
mail@schulz-und-schulz.com
www.schulz-und-schulz.com

Prof. Ansgar Schulz Dipl.-Ing. Architekt BDA DWB
Prof. Benedikt Schulz Dipl.-Ing. Architekt BDA DWB
Matthias Hönig Dipl.-Ing. Architekt
Dominik Schürmann Dipl.-Ing. Architekt BDA

Mitarbeiter/Working team: Christoph Untch, Christian Wischalla, Jana Unbehauen, Sarah Ahner, Elisa Thänert, Julian Lengert

Architekten + Generalplaner GmbH
Ronny Neumann Dipl.-Ing. Architekt BDA
Weststraße 2
D-08523 Plauen
Tel. +49-3741-280440
kontakt@neumannarchitekten.de
www.neumannarchitekten.de

Bearbeiter/Person in charge: Roger Neumann

Ausstellungsplanung/Exhibition planning
KOCMOC.NET GmbH
Marienplatz 1
D-04103 Leipzig
www.kocmoc.net

Photograph/Photographer
Gustav Willeit
I-39036 La Villa In Badia, BZ
www.guworld.com

Tragwerksplanung und Bauphysik/Structural engineering and building physics
Mathes Beratende Ingenieure GmbH
D-09112 Chemnitz

Heizungs-, Lüftungs- und Sanitär-Planung/Heating, ventilation and sanitary planning
Dr. Schlott und Partner GmbH
D-08056 Zwickau

Elektrotechnische Planung/Electrical engineering
Ingenieurgesellschaft Lachmann-Dominok mbH
D-08606 Oelsnitz/Vogtland

Thermische Bauphysik, thermische Isolierung und Energiebilanzierung/Thermal building physics, thermal insulation and energy balancing
GWT-TUD GmbH
D-01067 Dresden

Bauakustik, Raumakustik und Schallimmission/Building acoustics, room acoustics and sound immission
Akustik Bureau Dresden
D-01219 Dresden

Freianlagen/Outdoor facilities
Öko-Plan Bauplanung GmbH
D-08523 Plauen

Rohbau/Building shell
SP Bau GmbH
D-08485 Lengenfeld (Vogtland)

Dach und Zimmerei/Roof and carpentry
Thomas Knoll Dachdeckermeister
D-08626 Adorf/Vogtland
Andre Stark Zimmerei
D-08258 Siebenbrunn

Starkstrom/High-voltage current
Elektrotechnik Plauen
D-08523 Plauen

Schwachstrom/Low-voltage current
B+M Sicherheitstechnik Plauen GmbH
D-08527 Plauen

Pfosten-Riegel-Fassade und Fenster/Post-and-beam façade and windows
Crottendorfer Tischlerhandwerk GmbH
D-09474 Crottendorf

Sanitär und Heizung/Plumbing and heating
Andreas Johann GmbH
D-08645 Bad Elster

Lüftung/Ventilation
Neubert GmbH
D-09619 Sayda

Trockenbau/Drywall
Trocken- und Akustikbau Muck GmbH
D-08468 Reichenbach im Vogtland

Schlosserarbeiten/Locksmith work
Meiser Vogtland OHG
D-08606 Oelsnitz/Vogtland

Innentüren und Tischlerarbeiten/Interior doors and carpentry
Oertel Möbelwerkstätten GmbH & Co. KG
D-08496 Neumark im Vogtland

Naturstein/Natural stone
Protect Bau Stemmler GmbH
D-08485 Lengenfeld (Vogtland)

Estrich/Screed
Rascha Bau
D-09356 St. Egidien

Bodenbeläge/Flooring
Raumgestaltung Plauen GmbH
D-08527 Plauen

Malerarbeiten/Painting
Maler GmbH Reichenbach
D-08468 Reichenbach im Vogtland

Beschilderung/Signature
Heerlein Werbetechnik GmbH & Co. KG
D-10249 Berlin